DUNGENESSQUE

DUNGENESSQUE

RON CHARACH

George Amabile, Editor

Signature EDITIONS

Acknowledgments
Poems in this collection have appeared in the same or slightly different form in the following journals and literary publications: *Arc, Descant, event, The Fiddlehead, The Globe and Mail, Grain, The Lancet, The Medical Post, Parchment, Poetry Toronto, Prairie Fire, Prism International, Quarry* and *Queen's Quarterly.*

"Just Someone O.K." appeared in the anthology about jealousy, *The Third Taboo,* published by Wolsak and Wynn.

"A Late Entry to the Contest for the Best Poem about *Il Duce*'s Hands" appeared in the anthology *Vintage 92* published by Sono Nis Press.

Two key images in "Prize Poem with Animals" are from prize-winning poems by Patricia Young and Elisabeth Harvor.

"Crab" excerpt from *Mean* by Ken Babstock. Reprinted with permission from House of Anansi Press.

The author is grateful for thoughtful editing provided by Susan Ioannou and series editor George Amabile.

Cover design by Steven Rosenberg/Doowah Design.
Photo of Ron Charach by Irving Posluns.
Printed and bound in Canada by AGMV Marquis Imprimeur Inc.

We acknowledge the support of The Canada Council for the Arts and the Manitoba Arts Council for our publishing program.

Canadian Cataloguing in Publication Data

Charach, Ron
Dungenessque

Poems.
ISBN 0-921833-76-8

I. Title.

PS8555.H39834D85 2001 C811'.54 C2001-900260-2
PR9199.3.C4727D85 2001

Signature Editions, P.O. Box 206, RPO Corydon, Winnipeg, Manitoba, R3M 3S7

to Dr. Heinz Kohut

1913–1981
Vienna–Chicago

For hours I gawked at plasticky joints,
spotted, knobbed claws, and
wispy ferns at the mouth, how the sea's lens made
the shells swell, shimmer 'til
perspective was gone and their name
had washed up on my tongue—*Dungeness, Dungeness.*
The boy I was edged closer to them,
brine-spattered, waterlogged, less.

—from "Crab"
by Ken Babstock

Contents

Renovation

The Uncaffeinated Life

Epilogue

Prologue: Advisement

Advisement

Declining to do her yoga stretches in the nude
(what would be served, but an audience
and a draft wafting around loose baseboards)
she taunts:
If you need excitement,
put animals into your poems.

Last night I wanted her.
But I'll do anything to avoid pleading.
I opened a novel. Though I'm not content to sniff
at the base of artificial rocks and trees
for cleverness, I'm willing to suck
the marrow from every word.

These days, coffee goes straight for my heart,
my thighs grow thinner,
and no escape route on the horizon.
I pine for my former five/fifty mile,
wood chips on the secluded track
smelling of wet dog
(now that my sheltie, with malformed hip,
no longer runs like the wind.)
I mourn thick tomes unopened on bookshelves
whose dust has the feel of hypocrisy.

When I visit the emeritus rabbi's fabled library,
floor-to-ceiling, on rollers, his walls of antique books
like tidal waves could crush the senior reader,
were it not for a board he inserts to part them.
He holds up pages from ancient manuscripts,
books on alchemy and witchcraft,
Malleus Maleficarum,
the sciences of their day.

Let me show you also, he adds,
my brother Maurice's works;
etchings, oils, watercolours, sculptures in stone...
Maurice is very ill now, but once
he had a true genius for capturing birds.
If you too crave excitement,
have you considered placing
birds in your *vers libre*?

Prize Poem with Animals

for Patricia Young and Elisabeth Harvor

A poem that takes a prize should feature an animal,
perhaps an inspired chimpanzee clasping the top of her head,
improvising with an umbrella in a rainstorm
at the bottom of the Olduvai Gorge;
at least a faint scent
permeating the frantic search for a child
lost in a horse pavilion.

Al Purdy transformed a landscape
with caribou horses,
Elizabeth Bishop hatched a man-moth
from a newspaper misprint for "mammoth."

Through my own world
a people-pleasing, beadwork-squeezing sheltie named Buttons
gallops, and the mechanically nodding iguana, Pedro,
who, since he turned inexplicably orange,
charges his cage whenever his owner's mom approaches
lashing his tail and hissing,
childless by choice, childless by choice...

There are few horses or cows,
no chimeras, not even the shadow of a quetzal.
But the green-and-yellow budgie, Pierrot
flew through my manic aunt Leah's hanging ferns
"wherever in Eden he pleases,"
and her naughty third Burmese,
"Regina de la Farbotnik de Catkowitz Da Toid."

From so limited a bestiary
few prizes are possible,
although when I review
"A Late Entry to the Contest for the Best Poem about *Il Duce*'s Hands,"
I spot a caged gorilla peering
from behind the infamous brow and rubber lip.
The subject of my work remains
the human animal, ill-prized,
and the four-seasoned human face.

The Spectre

The Spectre

Masking the Terror

Behind the picture window
his mother stroked his hair,
in full view of his classmates;
they would never let him forget it.
"What did the others get?"
He brought home the highest grades,
played with an uneasy passion;
but the grades and the roles in operettas were
foretold; report cards
were read on arrival
and signed, each blending in
with the others: his family
was an audience. He refused
to wear spectacles
and could see his classmates down the road
long after they saw him.
He borrowed his father's glasses
to imitate foreign teachers
for the relatives.

At home alone
he searched through empty drawers,
behind doors, under bedspreads
looking for talismans,
the lost toy,
a soldier perhaps,
missing in action under a mountain of fluff.
He would arrange the figures in parades:
human, animal,
human, animal, animal, animal, human,
and then collapse the line.

At four
it would seem they switched dogs on him;
the first one had a bad heart
and couldn't run;
the second: same breed
but a bit smaller

and it ran like the wind;
Mother swore it was still
Sparky.

In need of mirrors,
the corrective sheen
of soothing fantasies
on long walks by the edge of the lake,
he would gaze out to the line of prairie
at the sun
going down to his orders;
but resentment reared its head
inside a filled-out adult
without substance:
the hollow Easter bunny
whose curves disappoint
from the first head-lopping bite.

Was there a hole for the worm to exit?
Because his step was inert
he took to wearing
boots with two-inch heels,
taps for a resonance,
and masked his terror
that death would come
in the middle of life.

At fourteen he set out to meet girls.
He had lucky lips, but would speed through partings
with subdued red hellos
in a crowd.

He forced himself out
into adult life;
learned the muscles in his neck.
A sense of never looking right
with no relief till the night walks
home from The Great Hall.
Other young men respected him;
a sense of his sentence on the rack,
did they imagine a scream?

Haughty,
he read the letters,
breathed deeply at the praise of peers;
If only they knew
how their admiration nourished him,
even if the legs trembled
as they bore the spectre out on walks,
arms feigning a martial swing
and the abdomen tightening
whenever he was stopped,
and forced to reveal
his terrified,
terrifying eyes.

WORDS WITH THE MARIANA TRENCH

Who expects to find you
yawning beneath Micronesia
just north of the Caroline Islands;
every word that locates you
rings with poetry. And yet you are
a thorax of cold black rock,
an Everest pulled through from the top,
taunting ambitious fools
lowered into you in cages
hooked to ropes as thick as wrists,
but thin as spider-web
to your six thousand fathoms,
is it more?
For you eat their sonar
and send back no signs.

You are the last objective correlative
the great depression
at once receptive and forbidding,
and what insight
from the flickering lamps
of your lost divers.

The gulf
that cuts between the hemispheres
of fat and nerve and fluid,
the inner Mariana of those convoluted ranges,
knows no light around the thin limb
that enforces the passage from right to left
to right again.

A young boy dreamed of filling you,
his thin soul spreading like a vapour.
But you were too real.
You'd freeze a vapour to its breather,
taking him and his fantasy
as an afternoon snack,
keeping your evenings free
for me.
I know
the ideals that you crush make you softer,
send shivers through your tortuous walls
till you moan and reconsider.

So I guard my reasons well;
as one would polish his harpoon in the morning sun,
test instruments of physics in a windless lagoon.
You'll know when I dive in, Mariana,
and you'll light up the Pacific
with a delirious welcome home.

The Ganges

My third night in the warm study,
the tiffany lamps transforming
the books themselves;
on cured animal skins
their titles in red and silver and gold,
resins;
pens and folders scattered about the rolltop desk,
with a clear space around your picture
like a space in my mind.
I reach for the portfolio
that leans at the desk, bloated

and straining at its large gold zipper,
when I come upon a smell
that won't blend with the musty rays
of books and sweat-worn leather;
the smell of my body in the room.
The portfolio drops from my hands
and I startle
at the sight of your picture.
Alone at my desk.
Somewhere inside these books
a cluster of words to describe you,
a chapter about great rivers and their deltas...

How many worlds am I removed from you
your bright face mirrored in the tiger's eyes,
a taste of your fleeting smile in his teeth.
He smiles at me,
not an animal smile;
unapproachable
as the Ganges.

The Man Who Cheats the Company

The words of the greats
disgusted him.
He would rather bleat and squeal
than be a vessel,
one more processor
on the milk run of knowledge.
How far he was
from the oily ones who smiled for their bosses,
the Company people
launching tiny salvos
from behind the rules.
Now that he was boss
he cringed when they nodded
and showed him as much tooth as they dared.
He would sooner bite into tinfoil
than be one of them,
though he was nothing himself.

Then she appeared,
her head slightly averted
as her body moved closer.
Turning him like a tap
with her walk, her smile,
the feline postures
of her sleep,
her wide-legged cotton suits
up which a hand could slide
straight to the warm wet root,
easing into her slender body
with a sweet guilt
that washed away boredom.
His sins called out for a temple in flesh,
towering over the man
who cheats the company.

He threw open the hold of his emotions
with no need to please.
With ease
she had primed him for a change;
He no longer lived for important mail,
or craved sleep,
or stared at his throat in the mirror
for signs of a heartbeat.
He watched her now;
she was filling him in,
from within.

The Three-piece Man in a Serious Suit

So now I sleep when the others do?
How far from that extravagant boy I once was
chasing my red prairie sun
behind the clouds,
shearing glaciers from the sides of mountains
with my mighty boot.

I should think well of her;
she helped roll the gauze across my eyes,
chloroform for the fool within;
I could hide him away for years.

No need now for the dotted-line form,
to be the bird that casts no shadows.

And if she dies,
look for a woman to love less…

Under skin and the roof of sky he took stock:
all he had were his ideals;
whoever has less has nothing more
than supermarket meat
and is more hollow than I am.

The table was set,
and he reached for the wine,
his hand sliding 'round the goblet like a viper.
Then his lips widened into a smile,
and the smile spread
to hers.

As Foreign Couples Rise

As Foreign Couples Rise

The corporate world continues its plan;
thirty journals arrive each day
with titles I abhor.
Chemicals swell the foreign rivers
of my mind,
then you tip my balance with the phone;
you invite me
but refuse to say where.

So I walk to any restaurant
and look for what you like:
a ceiling,
fans to cut the air in quadrants,
a bar with a large grey man
who weaves his dollars into a suit,
glass tables ringed with beer mugs,
single voices rising through the crowd-buzz
Not here. Sit here.
Perhaps a menu
as foreign couples rise;
nothing but Moroccan lamb
and eighty types
of grain, announcing:

Patrons will not be served.

The first portion of every meal is a choice.

When it finally arrives
it will look like something...aspic,
and there I will sit,
transparent as the table,
my waiter looking generic, bored.
Leaving.
To home in on your huge brick building
rising up in purring red verticals.
Pay phones close enough
to use in the softening up.

If this country would appear in your lobby,
ringing your nameplate
and staring at the buzzer

who would let it in?
Certainly I wait for well over an hour,
too proud to catch the door before it bites shut
whenever a red-eyed neighbour leaves.
Listening for static on the system, signs of you
reticent,
how can you disappoint
such a blind and faithful
search?

Squeezing the Barbarians

Three birthdays after our break-up
what do you buy me? Visigoth goblets
for a hairier man than you
would ever order.
Thanking me for anything I tell you
you hadn't already known,
yet resenting my advantage of "a few extra years"
over wine I handle well.

You should have checked inside your cool hand
before your thin white fingers squeezed;
my heart was an artichoke,
pale yellow
in a sauce of palm grease and melted nerves:
YOU NEVER FELT MY PAIN FOR TEN SECONDS
And I will neither soak my brain in brine
nor squeeze barbarians for stories
of how you've become
one of them.

I Like a Picture to Flatter

"What do you want me to do,
lose my estrogen advantage, grab my chest,
stop breathing; and that will be that?"

More than likely I'll beat you to it,
trembling between sweaty sheets after weeks
of your long bedside looks.
Tears will pour till I'm in shock
and they send for a chaplain
(will they know to make it a rabbi?)
He'll ask you to leave
because you're distressing me —
Imagine, leaving me to argue to the end
with some stiff-necked man of god
even as your selfy voice comes streaming
beneath the swollen door:
Rob, Honey, Answer if you're still alive,
Say that you forgive me!

That's when I start to second-guess
my house-husband skills
all these gentle words I put out like gas
when I'm weak-kneed or just this side of sick.
YOU SOLD ME THIS EDSEL-FLEET
OF EMOTIONS!
by scattering about pictures
(mostly bad, you're ambushed
by the light).
Before we met I would always
shred my bad ones,
like flakes of silver off a mirror.
I like a picture to flatter
its way to the perpetual,
till no one can describe it
or mouth at it
promises.

DUNGENESSQUE

Dungeness, Washington, The Olympic Peninsula

Crack me open like a crab
amused at the strange soft fur along my shell.
Tour my body
find the emotional limits,
dredge my character
for small signs of pretense;
you know they're there.
Haven't others glimpsed claws
beneath my hands?
You listen so closely,
stretching out my present against my past
on a long net,
laying bare...

Boil me live
in a scalding cauldron
like you would a crab,
turning your head
as the claws fold in silently
and you wait for the soft clicking sound.
You can eat me tonight
or tomorrow, or the next night.
because the cooking's done;
all that's left is to analyze
what can and can't be consumed.
Tomorrow you and your analyst
will pick through the bowl of white flesh
from my brittle compartments.
There may be a joke or two,
"Who'd have thought the old boy
would have so much meat in him?"

Burn Ward

These people did not suffer their losses by degrees;
the suit peeled, and a million bright red dots
of vessels-on-end were suddenly exposed.
It happened in a matter of seconds.

Could my charms have dried up so quickly?
One morning, waking alone,
pains ripping up and down my back like flames
father's death a halo of molten lead,
feelings seeping through the gauze of character,
I could think only of refuge,
of finding a healthy lover from the past
to trick me into surviving.
That morning, unable to rise from the bed,
muscles like dry dough on the bones, I knew
the wells were tapped.

You go to Emergency when you can summon no resources.
You present at a hospital desk, and though the burn ward
would do the trick, they admit you
to a ward where people on pills
walk their problems down halls.
But when the old resources are mirages,
things you loved and can still describe,
what is there to do but stay awake in the desert
hoping to spot them again, by trying harder to believe.
Can you find balance in the wheel of life
when you flew from a center to the edge of a rim
in seconds?

JUST SOMEONE O.K.

Who's going to walk the frozen seas
of your moods
if not me;
only I take such haunting.
Those winter nights
we left the country parties
in silence,
you searching like a pilot
while I struggled with the snowed-in roads
and tried to read the signs.
I'd pull to the shoulder
and ask you what I'd done
(assuming it was me)
and you'd answer,
like a pothead watching your children play;
then disappear,
keeping—was it warm, or merely free of me.
I could understand if you'd thought about me
with headaches or the old doubts
and more;
But so often: "Someone—just *someone, O.K.!*
No one you know."
Our history left you chained
to something dead.
There were times on my patrol
that my anger shot up with
dragonfly eyes:
Consider the ditch,
or an oncoming pair of brights,
something to take you,
maybe break
your train of thought.

Venus Betraying

A fine portrayal of you
sashaying into the sauna
manned by your two gay friends, naked
under the black and white dragon kimono
I bought you.

You lie a-belly,
and lift and expose yourself to the halogens
after months of letting me watch you
only in dim light.

Two clones who are "into other men"
take turns massaging your in-
completely perfect parts
—all the more delicious!

Wriggling on the bleached wood,
half of you tensing, then the other,
then the first again,
how succulent, to lean back and study for hours!
A servicing Don Juanita supports your waist
while his buddy kneads away at one sweet loaf at a time,
more low-budget Swedish than shiatsu,
the relaxation so total that you let loose,
and apologize, "Excuse me..."

"Excuse us," they answer,
with what fantasies?
That you're a heavy-set friend?
Who knows what use they have for an hourglass form,
though they're said to adore its
impersonation on the stage.

Are you adored, or are you trifled?
Could you not have received
the same from me?

But you were so deeply pickled in wine
when we made love, defending
against my interests,
the latent picket fence and stroller intentions.

So now, my love, for you,
this farewell,
bearing no other motive
than to return the prideful shame
in kind.

Organ Meats

The yellow arm that froze me on the run,
someone autumn could not cover,
his arm the colour of parched leaf,
product of a mind otherwise engaged;
this aching heart that lunges behind bars,
it too tilts. These lips
a'crackin' for a midnight kiss,
vague memories of us locked smile to smile,
rolling over each other on the lawn
with the take of organ meats.

This is the night when she can smell the escape-butts,
when Miss Bombay says her four foreign words in the hallway,
perfunctory as a rear view,
when her little Mishkin yaps by
and is *not* named after the prince.
This is a night for spotting the dramatic,
the disembodied, like the tiny head
on a man playing golf,
or an instant heirloom,
thirteen sweatbands
stitched to a compelling
American flag;

Slowed to a walk
this last quarter-mile,
lead in the legs up the final stairs,
two-pound weights around each wrist
as we ease in the slightly bent key
and burst in on her,
Surprise!...

This *would* be the night
that she bolts.

WHO?

Who but a woman
can leave a washroom smelling sweeter
than when she entered?
Who but a Holocaust survivor
refuse the camouflage of medication rather than switch off
truths too terrible to let go?
And who but you, Love,
could discard me
like so much chopped liver in a napkin,
tilting the mirror at me, to reveal
little Adolph in his dress of blue.

A Late Entry to the Contest for the Best Poem about *Il Duce's* Hands

I avoid my Reflection in shop Windows.
Some Mornings I wake up
powerful enough to pull Eagles
from the Sky, to set my naked Skull
against a Bear's.
Yet even then the Mirror reflects
"vigorous little Man."
This is Tyranny, that limits Desire,
that stifles Appetite

To hold an enormous Crowd in the Piazza for *Hours,*
craning to salute an ancient Symbol
that faces *every Way at once...*
To vow *We will eat the Bodies of your attacking Troops!*
to finally display *all* the Teeth,
even those in the crocodile Cortex
those rotary Blades of the Amygdala
that flash through the Brain
at three and four and five A.M.

Duce, tell us: Where can the Body store such Energy?
Not in a protruding lower Lip or a forward-thrusting Jaw,
these are but *Emblems* of a great hurt Pride.
No. To witness the Feat we must lower our Eyes
and gaze at where the Furies weigh Anchor:
these broad-fingered Miracles
that shake the Pacifist to his rattling Core,
your two best Friends and ours
your powerful, empowering Hands.

Ruining Teflon

MORNING POEM WITH ANIMALS

Your dry white wine has sanded my brain smooth.
The Japanese beetle that winds through canals
and plays the eardrum after mating
heads for the wet spot on the sheets
like some horny little joker.
Waking to an unlikely relief,
I let loose into the pedestal sink a litre of liquid gold,
Irving Layton-style.

"Why did you leave me?"
asks the sightless veiny viper
curved unrelentingly upward,
refusing to conform to the task at hand,
rendering the whole performance a messy spray,
like you,
or my life
as a juggler of near-weightless balls,
who diverts pressure from the heart,
that overburdened bag of tricks
more full of surprises
than a hospital ER.

Here, boy! Cummon, boy!
Together let's once more miss the mark, me
and my arrow, the untrainable pointer,
a man's best, last-remaining
friend.

Our Pointless Occupation

What did you do leave your secret life under a tree somewhere?
We go to bed and what do you talk about? General Foods.
What somebody said at the office, for Christ's sake.
Am I supposed
to beat off under a bush just so I can keep my eyes closed?
You, with your back parked against my wall, saying
Use your words, Roddy. Use your words.
Yet dripping around in a terry cloth
in the name of what? *Comfort?*
I can't fight on these terms;
when the hanging man shakes, I shake.
This room messed with hands is my room.
I therefore reclaim both halves of the bed;
a thank-you card for whatever you snuck away:
the downwardly milky tears;
lint-trapping eyes at the center of our bodies:
my pushy anatomy,
your widely touted grin and pout;
the bed-and-board of our pointless occupation.
Things would be so much different at your office, I know.

Ruining Teflon

Whenever the negative wave overtakes him
and his forehead hatches into a long bead,
and all this brought on
by the too-swift surfacing
into a world of damage,
and there is no couch from which to holler whoa!
and nothing but a wife in the next room
as deep in her life and her sleep
as he is tentative in his,
then he takes to the dishes for an easy go with factuals,
always saving the Teflon for the end,
for the "I can still be gentle" topper
to a life rage
that she finds pointless as a daily note:
Please remember
the smooth sheen of the efficient
is easily destroyed.

A Homily on Ripeness

Tumours do not grow in stained wood hallways,
nor have they the weight of antique furniture.
The Persians are so indentured
that coasters have *had* to be used.
Noises out of the complex basement
have coughed these past three months,
and worry us
that destiny's white arm will surprise us
under the stairs.
Every night the right to property
must be debated, even though
the finish on the table is scratched
and the lamp has gone too far,
with a bulbous base
to cover its devices.
For now the wallpaper has not buckled:
"You and I have done well,"
says the sofa that cost us parts of our bodies,
new ways we might have improvised
for reaching other bodies.
We both thin out here
and we thicken; soon the year-old turnip
that weighs nothing
will be a homily
on ripeness.
"Confess,"
says the fireplace
that has no cradle, no brass daughter
and can never be fired,
"Confess that you find me empty."

Downstairs
inside a painted rag
a centipede pens a suicide note,
with a plenitude of dusty legs
to warn us

to keep out the light.

Somewhere Half-forgotten

Somewhere
half-forgotten
though unforgettable, lost inside the debates
on exactly when and where to start him
in junior kindergarten,
somewhere far beyond the lists
of daycares in church and temple basements, rec centres, private homes,
unlikely corporate
headquarters—

something elemental, like
that look of recognition he beamed
when Grandpa, away these past six months,
appeared
at the arch of the family room,
hair so silvery white and a smile so broad
you knew he wouldn't be footing the bills
or drawing up the game plan
for the next eighteen years.

They had nothing to do but react
to each other, to take
each other in
like the deep orange shine on a bay
meant for visiting.

The Mirror that Must Be on Standby

By the hallway mirror
one more obligatory jogger
peels off his soaked sweaters.
Blood rises
into the cisterns of his blotchy chest
where the hair has greyed and thickened.

She too needs his blood to keep moving
in front of the mirror,
on standby for her, should anything happen.

Their little ones shine in the den
watching carefully chosen tapes on the VCR,
blood and water and lymph moving
so smoothly they defy the melancholia
that lifted faces from grandparents, great-uncles and great-aunts
like so much frozen bark.

Quiet, one foot, the other,
he squeezes colour back into his toes
while an infra-red alarm
blinks on and off.

Seven times a year
they strip the mantle, and watch
thick dwarf candles
twist memorial flames
in glass.

Preparations

I am preparing for the privations of age
to avoid being massacred
like some old babushka jarred awake
by a machine-gun burst of nostalgic balalaika.

I review the films of Cassavetes and Bergman
to train for the snowdrifts
of too much and too little detail.

I study poems with long titles
and arrestingly simple lines—
Death of a Son, in a Mental Hospital, Age One,
in which Jon Silkin states,
"I have seen stones."

I am preparing for the sheer
surprises of age.
I too have seen stones.

The Unlikely Combines

Each day threatens
the mind with a fresh incursion;
the familiar bridge:
an enormous red combine about to leave the painting
and crush forward on the wall,
a hired hand wiping a sweaty brow:
"Torments of the Harvest."

Though I supply you with artfulness
you keep dredging me for
"a fundamental stash of seriousness,"
your suspicions flow like runners
down the late-night stairs,
your good judgment holds
like a bridge to safer contacts,
better times, soothing galleries.
But you are immured
in thoughtful approaches to the emotions,
a politic way of leaving the room
or tuning out muffled cries
whenever you catch me
"confounding"—

Tonight I need you
to hold open your green eyes
and look up as the unlikely combines:
white acoustic tile and an Algerian fan.

Renovation

Phoebe's Place Cards

On each place card she has sketched
a cousin's foot, a finger, a lap,
a navel, spiked hair,
the back of a ponytailed head
interwoven with a seasonal ornament:
straddling the bridge of a daughter's nose,
a miniature pony,
in thickets of punk hair, a mini-Santa,
while a bauble dangles from its wire
between another's lips.

We parents find our places by guessing
which body part belongs to whose child,
(the answer, in calligraphy, is clearly on the back).
The kids were thrilled to pose
for their cousin's darting marker-pens.
Like us, they now take their proper places,
card-carrying members
of an ornamental,
ordered world.

Rocks and Ages

At Mohonk Mountain House

Lawn bowling with Daniel
at his parents' Fiftieth,
while the kids explore the Shawangunk cliffs,
he tells me that once he too
nearly did his back in
—a slippage forward of the vertebrae
while wrestling in college.
His jet-black hair frames sculpted features
atop his black polo shirt and khakis.

We inhale the rich blend of Nature
and Nineteenth Century manufactured charm,
and watch old folks strolling the formal gardens,
or stooping under the boughs
of a hundred-year-old beech tree,
banyan of the North.
Some, less able, content themselves with a range
of room to porch to dining-room.

Daniel says, "This Mountain House has something for everyone,
from scrambling rocks to rocking chairs
—as they say, for the newly wed
to the nearly dead."
He hesitates in the sunlight,
as if something seized him by the jaw:
"I can't turn my head too quickly or I get dizzy,
the vision's often a blur."
Must be the MS he's been battling
almost two years now.

At Taughannock State Park

We take the blistering sunshine route
declining the shaded woodland path
favoured by our wives,
and follow the kids into the rushing stream.
Pocked rock beds quarried for slate
form miniature tide pools
the kids love to splash through.
Daniel informs me, "The 215-foot waterfall we'll reach at the end
was used as a film set for *Tarzan* in the Thirties.
The path the girls are taking was the road
they built for the film crews.
They attached ropes so he could swing across
from one end to the other."

Past a bend in the gorge there it tumbles,
its notch carved over millennia
into cliffs of jagged slate and crumbly shale,
bane of the rock climber.
Far ahead of the wading dads, the kids set a bristling pace,
romping across slippery rocks,
as we men measure our steps
and take our precious time.
When we finally catch up,
Daniel looks for a place to sit,
and adjusts his hat in the blinding sun.

In University

"Did you know that 'Fort Book' is sinking!"
my daughter exclaims airily.
"The architects of the Robarts Library
never allowed for the weight of the books!"

    I think of the University Athletic Center, "Fort Jock,"
    where a huge picture window lightens the bunker look,
    where we'd plod through snowdrifts
    to watch the firm splashing bodies
    of the women's swim team;
    where the building's exhaust still emits a waft of chlorine
    so heady it can lure back lapsed swimmers.

I tell her,
"I once knew the grand-daughter of the stone mason
who chiseled gargoyles into the walls of Trinity and Hart House."
To which she answers, "Cool."
I want to say,

    "I too was once an undergrad
    fresh as paint slapped across a wrought iron fence,
    waving my antennae at greatness:
    the bearded Master of Massey College Davies
    the elliptical media seer McLuhan
    Victoria College's clean-shaven sage Northrop Frye"
    —as stellar a cast
    as writer Atwood and Nobel laureate Polanyi
    are to her.

I'm wondering, though,
after handing her the first of many cheques,
can these monuments
really nourish so many youthful souls
who keep upping the ante with heady expectations?
What kind of foundation will she get here,
one of bedrock, or of shifting plans,
when she marches off after four years
sporting mortarboard and tassel,
clutching her hard-earned roll
of inscribed paper?

Comet Soup

After four throbbing days
of sinuses ballooning my skull,
I grab raincoat and umbrella
and risk pneumonia for Pho Hung.
The owner can spot a desperate diner
and summons his daughter to serve me.

Hunched over my meal in a neighbourhood
without dry cleaners on every corner,
I inhale the vapours of seething comets
trailing long slippery tails through a universal broth,
scoop deeper for ghost-balls with a porcelain spoon concave its full length
and pierce their rice-noodle chambers
for a starburst of peppery pork
that steams open long-sealed passages,
suffusing my Diasporic brain with Eastern spices and MSG,
unbattening the hatches
of all eight teeming berths, till my eyes pour, unsure
if this is therapy or sin.

The Body on the Subway

I'm hanging from a strap like a side of beef,
when a tsunami of thought erupts,
nearly hurls onto the lap of a newspapered
three-piece-suiter.
A lithe Asian beauty
in an open cashmere cardigan
reluctantly steps aside
to let pass a bowed elder of her tribe;
he drags behind a bundle-buggy overloaded
with heavy bags of rice.

This morning, what headlines!
"World's fastest man severs Achilles tendon,"
"Young Chinese ballerina achieves ineffable beauty
by having eyes done."

My own eyes squeeze to crow's feet,
recalling titles that celebrate the body's genius—
Perfect Health,
Ageless Body, Timeless Mind,
Perfect Timeless, Priceless —

if buffeted by rattling coughs and fever blisters,
"the runner's knee as the new back,"
novel constricting outlet syndromes,
daredevil skirmishes with gravity,
as women install and remove implants,
pare noses, inflate lips, wax legs and upper lip,
suck abdominal fat up plastic hoses,
owners of bodies everywhere
fleeing their ancestors—

The grey metal pole grows warm and clammy,
so many have clenched it before me;
I fumble through my jacket for a pen.

After the Election

Another provincial election drawn to a close,
what consoles better than to harvest sticks
from the candidates' signs, and, with burlap,
nurse a rhododendron or two through the winter?
But someone's beaten me to it!
Streets show no evidence of men and women
who put names and reputations on the line.
Only a lone black-on-orange, socialist sign
graces a tiny private lawn
behind a wrought iron fence.

"Well, hello!" she greets me warmly,
a handsome woman in matronly grey,
as I yank the sign from its staples.
"You must be Freda's brother-in-law.
Darn shame, four more years of Tory rule, eh?"
"It is," I mumble,
"but actually, I'm not a brother-in-law,
er, I'm just collecting sticks,
you know, for use in the garden—"

"*You bastard*, get the *hell* off my property!"
shouts this mild-mannered mother of two—who knows—three.
"And leave that signpost where you found it!"
Guarding the back of my head,
I edge across city grass to the curb
where my Toyota idles, trunk open,
and with a schoolboy whine
retort, "But everyone does it!"
wondering if she'll expose me
next time she scrutineers.

Renovation

"This kitchen has to go."

After forty years, the cupboard doors, with hinges
known only to the ancients, threatened
to come off in our hands.
Heavy, reluctant pull-out drawers
menaced an unstable back,
while "These days drawers glide in and out
smooth as butter."
A wedged silver tray became immured,
patterns on the linoleum floors were faint memories.

Natural maple cabinets have been chosen,
golden blonde veneer on pressed wood,
"stronger than the real thing."
The trustworthy double sink will soon be scrapped.
The brown pearl granite
and tumbled marble back-splash, now on order,
will outlive us, and our kids.

More physical men
with better backs at forty, even fifty,
haul drywall, breathe fumes,
and grapple with fridge and stove.
One evening, during a lull in operations,
two cleanly broken potsherds shine through,
threaded with black straps
that might have bound the wrists of a Samson.
Their identical smooth surfaces
are not clay, after all,
but molded rubber,
used by carpenter, painter, or flooring-man,
whatever lord of the quarter-round now invited
inside our palace gates.

At the Temple during Days of Awe,
the senior rabbi jostled pillars of the community
by condemning the diversion of funds
from good works to kitchen cabinetry.
In today's *Globe*, a man recounts

how he renovated his face:
eyelids trimmed, chin angle adjusted,
fat harvested from his thighs
to realign his cheeks,
an ear pinned.
"He should have tried some nice glasses,
maybe a beard."

After four weeks of chaos,
there will be four more.
Disarmed, we flee with our children up north,
leaving behind oriental carpets tied in bundles.
How many workmen have copies of our key?

"The nicest thing about having a modern kitchen,"
I tell my Princeton-trained wife of eighteen years,
"is not only will the food taste better,
but neither of us will ever die."
She feigns a grimace.
Has she overlooked
the small cairn of knee-guards
I mistook for pottery
beside the condemned fridge?
Can she not hear the whir and whine
as loyal appliances prepare to surrender
to their betters in stainless steel?

Courtesy of Plastic

One summer afternoon
courtesy of plastic
I set out to buy perfect lava
at Canadian Tire,
paying double for the geometry
when crumbled rock would do just as well.
Could not the same fire be lit
by the derelict who frequents yards that back onto the ravine,
the hungry soul who eyes my double gas grill
on below-zero nights?

Later that evening
from inside my upper-middle bathysphere
instead of watching him raccooning,
I switch off the Japanese lantern floodlights
and let him see in.
Beckoning him
with a persuasive finger,
I overlook his "Who, *me*?" scowl
and greet him at the door
like long-lost family from overseas,
have him peel his Salvation Army greatcoat
which he needs more than ever.
Holding my breath, I give him the complete tour.
Feel this, smell this, notice these, how they all match.
Lest he collapse on me,
I sit him, still silent,
in the family room
on a well-Scotchgarded chair.

But when he rolls down his matted socks
feet so motley gruesome appear
they eclipse the Persian rugs.
As he rubs them, still looking away from me
my heart bleeds, "Forgive me."
I resort to a kind of lava-speak:
"Forgive all of us, in such identical shape,
who distribute our warmth evenly
to family and close friends,

forgive our ability to make a go
of this indifferent world."
Holding up my smooth hands to him,
hands of a hobbyist, in benediction,
I intone the *que sera:*
"How many sacrificial lines will crack
my final face?
Can I remain true to my childhood ethic
that all inherited wealth is evil?
Will the day come when I can say, "Enough,
this is wealth enough."
Or will the spiral accelerate
to lasso an even glitzier
chandelier, still more momentous
visits to the bank
to protect the investment,
slap another coat on the Tudor,
service the Jag, the Mercedes and the Jeep,
with every last accounted dollar
well spoken for?

"Help me climb down," I beseech him
as he stuffs his bristly cheeks with chocolate almonds
and starts screwing around with the remote control.
"Help me off the treadmill,
remind me I already own
too much."

But now he's into the Chivas,
one of my kids is up
for a late-night piss
and the earlier invitees in the upstairs guest room
are going at it great guns,
the whole world is clicking so smoothly
that I might as well try for some sleep.

I check with him a last time,
my unreformed,
oddly unimpressed bum,
and suggest he leave before I call 9-1-1.
"We're all bums," I reassure him,

handing him his wretched coat
and showing him the door
with courtesy, always a surprise
to a man in his position; courtesy
like the warm glow of a lava lamp,
something even a weary chip
of plasticized rock
can sustain.

All My Uncles were Crazy

for Mich

Even mon oncle Jean-Marc,
remembered for driving his four-by-four
straight through a swollen creek,
who feared neither man nor beast,
and tramped into deep Eastern Township woods
on drunken hunting expeditions,
cringed at being alone in the dark.

Once, at the edge of the lake,
high in the trees, to discourage bears,
he and Papa constructed a house.
Dreading voiding at night,
Jean-Marc insisted they install
a heavy porcelain toilet
he'd brought in the back of his pick-up,
rigged to a long drainage pipe.

To hoist it into the trees,
Jean-Marc tied his rope end to the old launch,
and as the horsepower revved down the lake
the white throne rose up on its pendulum
narrowly missing Papa
—SMASH, SMASH—three days to build
and the tree house was gone.
Limp rope trailing on the water,
all night Jean-Marc circled the lake
trembling at its black depths
and leering rocks.
Every now and then in thick joual
he cried to Pa, *"Claude! Claude!*
Is okay I come back now?"

But Papa looked down his gun barrel.
"Tabernacle! Ah'm gonna kill you!"
and fired another round.

Papa and Jean-Marc, both gone.

The Trap

The mousetrap's feeding platform
was a faux slice of Swiss cheese
emitting a faint chemical smell. I slid it
behind the cottage's water heater.

Next morning, the trap had moved nearly a foot,
dragged by a mouse still waving her forelegs,
lower back crushed
by the lightning stroke of Victory design.
An eager fox lived under our cabin,
but to such tooth-and-claw agony
I could not abandon my prey.

Holding the trap, I immersed her
head-first into the toilet bowl.
The little jaws made three or four gulping motions.
I waited half a minute
until the thrashing forelegs stilled.

Well after I was certain death had arrived,
I withdrew the trap
and let the stiffened corpse fall
into the plastic bag lining our bathroom basket,
then covered it with paper, hidden
from kids who once kept "fancy mice" as pets.

I have deprived
our too-friendly fox of a leisurely meal.
I fear a mouse's death,
back problems catastrophized
by some giant fate-sprung trap
followed by a baptism that makes me gasp,
no matter how swiftly its blessing arrives
to spare me from being eaten alive.

Wha-*choo* worried about? says a familiar voice.
You're self-employed.

GIRL'S LEGS

On a moonlit, sub-zero night,
walking my sheltie Buttons through the ravine,
we meet a black and white mutt named Tyler
and Alex, with unruly dirty-blonde hair,
round-faced as an overgrown kid
straight off a farm outside Kingston.

As the dogs start romping like old buds
their owners stamp feet to stay warm.
Alex wisecracks about "Chinese drivers."
I can guess he's not keen on Blacks or Jews
(I don't even think about gays),
but I tell him, "Hey, man, it's 2000,"
and he shrugs. "So, live and let live."
I know if I dropped in, his mom's place
would be rich with pet smells,
heaped with sweaty clothes and junk mail
proclaiming, "Hey, people fuckin' *live* here."

Loping up, a dog named Marlowe
—yes, after the writer—
growls at Tyler, but Buttons snaps him in line.
His owner's a stocky New Brunswicker named Eamon.
Like Warren Oates, but with more purpose to his ramble,
he tells how the cops Down East
chased him till he rolled his Mustang,
how a jutting rock wiped out his moped
along with recall of his first thirteen years;
how, more than once, in a local bar
serial killer Allan Legère drank beside him.

Alex wades in with a tale
about his cousin on a nearby dairy farm.
"I'd watch him dive off the dock into the lake,
one of his legs was more like a long stick or a bone.
He caught me starin', and said,
'It's a girl's leg. No muscle.
From me and my Honda losin' a fight
with an overpass. I was in hospital for weeks.
Could'a been worse, like one of them wishbone fractures
straight up the middle of the crotch.'"

Ouch!
My tales can't compete,
nor do I confess
I've been storking around myself
on scrawny legs since the day I could walk,
one side even more withered
thanks to a bad back.

That's no more his business
than what my dog gets for table scraps.
Besides, on this freezing night,
in thick corduroys and skiing long johns,
I feel untippable.
I'm not going to trade these two
their powerful country-boy legs
for amnesia, or too-thin gloves and no hat,
the kind of fatherlessness
that makes a guy come down over-hard
on the gentler side of the species.

Buttons and I veer away,
her tail whisks me a path through the night.
Out of earshot, I ask,
"Whatever becomes of us,
it's always Mom's fault, right?"
Buttons jumps up on her girl's hind legs
and as we pick up the pace,
she nips at my heels
all the long journey home.

The Uncaffeinated Life

A Portrait of My Father

Dad, it's me, the *klayner,*
your "little one"
(never mind the rude meaning of the term).
This morning from the last person's flush
a spectral white carnation
floated in the bowl,
three-ply, the sort of nicety for which you had little use;
it was never memorialized
in Twenties, Thirties and Forties songs
you so loved to sing.
It's like Hea-ven when I'm—near you!
It would be Para-dise—near you!
Once, you sang Louis-Prima-style
I-I-I ain't got No-body!
and a work mate chortled,
Sammy, you got body all right,
beeg body, har har har!

You stoked your insomnia with late-night Coke,
dressed only in what, years later, a patient of mine
termed "a wife-beater shirt,"
your pregnant belly barely supported
on tripod legs no thicker than my own,
in baggy white briefs so tattered
the undershirt's length was a mercy.

You would rather be remembered
dressed in a black CPR windbreaker
over a work shirt and well-creased olive pants,
crouching in the union photo
alongside the other baggage checkers.
You weren't heavy yet,
blood pressure was normal,
you hadn't started those pills
that turned your brain into a desert.
You had a pretty 27-year-old wife
(just a bit old for those days).
No wonder you were smiling, bright-eyed
beside Buchholtz, Prokopchuk and Rowdan
—not a Jew in the bunch, but work buddies

who didn't use "Jew" as a verb to your face
unless they'd had one too many.

Not buddies or mates, you and I
never tossed a ball back and forth,
—what older brothers were for—
even in the shallow lake's splashing contests
exchanging no more than a rare wave
during "peace treaties" I proclaimed,
hysterical with laughter.
You lolled silently nearby,
Monstro, a great pink whale
on his back,
catching your breath.

God rest you, Father,
who checked out at 56,
crooner, punster,
at times overmedicated monster,
hear the call of your deep-sea diver son
who navigated your obstacle course to manhood
and would replay the game of hit-and-miss
for a heartfelt hug at the end,
a sincere, if sloppy, kiss.

Blood Libel

"There's one problem marrying a pretty *shiksa:*
Sooner or later she turns into an old *goya.*"

In my mother's *shtetl*-speak, the spectre
is an embittered mate, transforming late
into the dreaded "*Anti-Semeet!*"
who, at the last moment, refuses to share
her family's Holocaust fate,
or, in another nightmare, flames into rage
when the inevitable child-support
payments are past due.

To those whose forebears were repeatedly libelled
—remember Mendel Beilis, accused
of draining the blood of Christian children
to stir into his wife's ceremonial matzoh—
perhaps a little libel comes easy.
(They were a couple who knew better
than to intermarry!)
Would my mother's words have sounded
nastier, more anti-female,
tripping off my father's lips?

If Orthodox enforcers of sexual apartheid
are more penitential,
have they greater transgressions
to repent?

What choice, for men who refuse to pray with women
lest they offend a jealous God,
who would never let their children play
with Diaspora resident aliens,
who curse free thinkers
as *m'shumeds,* treacherous converts,
enemies of the one
true tribe of Israel.

On a single point all Yiddish writers agree:
S'eez shver tzu zein a Yid in Goless.
It's hard to be a Jew in Exile.

Any easier, an old Jewess than an old *goya?*
It depends.
Is she a *greeneh* or a *geleh,*
a “greenhorn” or a third-generation “white one”?
Who is her chosen husband?
And what is his take on the rules
for those who do versus those who do not
cyclically bleed?

Unnatural Predators

One time too many.
A colleague's rhododendrons
have been nipped in the bud,
and buoyed on three martinis, he claims
he'd gladly drown a squirrel,
Disney tail and all,
just as he might a rat.

"A crow, of course, will eat a young squirrel,
the way a coyote will a small dog."
I picture my sheltie, Buttons,
hoisted aloft by the splendid murderous buzzard
in Wilbur's "Still, Citizen Sparrow"
or hauled down at the throat
by an agile, wilder relative,
although the raccoons and foxes in the ravine
shy away from my colleague's squirrels
and his walled-off garden in tony Forest Hill.

On Burrows' tattered boulevard,
my father loved to chatter back at the squirrels.
He nicknamed them "kuroliks,"
close to Kurelek, the prairie painter
some say was his own worst predator,
a man unknown to my working father.

The Canadian Pacific Railway
was the wolf that might one day tear poor Sammy,
by his secret Jewish roots,
from the Ukrainian Mikes and Steves
manning the dusty baggage room.
"*Then* how will you survive?"
He threatened his totemic brood:
mother hen, horse, and rabbit.

His taunt still sends me
digging down burrows to escape
the penurious fame of poetry.
True, I studied Medicine to help
people fight off natural predators,
but also dreamed of rising

swift as a garter snake
up the greased pole of the food chain
where nothing short of death
or unnatural ambition
could ever snatch me away.

Cornfields

I am not one to stand barefoot in cornfields,
warm wet earth easing between my toes,
watching for signs of the corn growing
—it springs up so quickly.
Nor have I hiked up highland roads,
squinting at hillsides
for a crop of ruined castles.
Yet visitors daily bring me accounts of such sightings,
needing help to touch down in their workaday lives.
Eyes tethered to their computer's screen-saver sky,
brains on automatic pilot, their instep
still aches for sandy beach and stony trail,
the ecstasy of mountains.

Guarding against The Father's arm
reaching down to grab the scruff of my neck
or shaking me till my legs go weak,
I toe a prairie line
of endless vistas.
Long ago I renounced
the blind alleyways of
motorcycle, sports car and downhill ski.
To my shame, not unhappily, I linger
by the bend of the Inner Thigh
like a pissing-fountain fisher boy
waiting for a miraculous bush
to flash blonde, brunette or redhead,
and grant me what he too pursued,
what we all pursue,
the inalienable scent and entry
into the warm wet earth
of deepest human nature.

Ant and Aphid

Along a cedar crosspiece on my garden gate,
they move past in deadly duet.
A carpenter ant lugs a bright green aphid,
its legs waving weakly in the breeze,
and climbs the thick stalk of ivy
to its nest under the warm wet eaves.

This tiniest of nature's victims,
does it leave descendants, a work history,
even if no clock was punched?
At its sudden violent passing
will there be testimonials,
or co-religionists
obsessively scouring the garden square
for signs of massacred remains?

Have not hired ladybugs
headstrong and pretty as gaily painted tanks
carried out such ethnic cleansing?

A red-winged songbird swoops down,
plucks both ant and prey from the ivy
and soars skyward
—a miraculous ascent?

This morning, awaking,
at once I knew I no longer had skin,
that everything and everyone who passed my way
would move me,
the world's pain as much as its beauty.

And look! The solar clematis
sprung up along the fence
are beaming apricot-white faces,
petals boldly unfurled,
determined as any natural thing
whose hours are numbered.

The Uncaffeinated Life

The uncaffeinated life is not worth living.

Why truck with existential extremists
who embrace a nervous life
to feel more aware?
No worse than whitewater adventurers
who shoot the rapids in blue and yellow rafts
emblazoned large with "CAMELS"
as if cancer sticks were a staple of training,
as well they may be.

Tonight I toss and turn
after coffee taken late at The Lombard,
the afterglow of a semi-tasteful "adult" film
repeating on me, unwelcome now,
the visuals nowhere near as good
as what one can arrange at home,
even if more extreme and yet,
when one travels alone...

in shallows, like this attempt at sleep,
a drugged contemplation of whatever drifts by.
I try to push off with a mantra:
the usual prairie grasses
alternating waves of light and shadow,
but what chance has mindfulness
against chocolate-covered espresso beans?

My thoughts turn to German POWS
exported to Medicine Hat, Alberta,
forced to build the local dam,
and to the orphaned Jewish teen
corralled with them for no reason
until a Jewish family from Toronto
stepped in to adopt him free.

I think of the Jew who became a Baptist
after marrying an American.
On his deathbed, he converted right back,
then phoned around frantically for relatives
still willing to carry his pall.

And I think of ambitious limo drivers
high on bennies
who allow the car ahead an eighth of a chevron
for every 10 kph of their flight.

My last attempt is a counting song:
Type A on coffee/neutralized by sleep,
Type A on coffee/neutralized by sleep,
the result, a yawn so deep
it would make a coffee-grower weep.

Three Buskers

In a station of the subway,
the smiling old Chinese
plays a mournful erhu and celestial flute,
while the exiled Russian with the violin
tackles Paganini between trains with a long black bow.

On the other side of the platform,
an overweight reformed alky
honks "Amazing Grace"
repeatedly on a sour horn,
relying on pity to fill his cup.

Near the exit, the man with dreadlocks
and limited talent plays and sings songs
meant for the dust-heap of pop musical history.
He stands harmlessly strumming an acoustic guitar,
subtly eyeing his near-empty hat,
but no one tosses him a wish,
for no one wants to call him
mon semblable or *mon frère.*

A Full Measure

Behind me, squeezes into the streetcar
a still smaller man.
"Mind the doors," the driver warns.
"You're in the way."
With a sheepish look, the man insists,
"I'm okay."
The driver barks,
"Isn't your head attached to your body?"
The doors snap shut.

Ahead of us
within pecking distance,
sits a blond woman in a Carpathian dress.
Atop her Afghan hat
perch two budgies, "Buzzie" and "Davie."
Are they alive? All riders are transfixed
as they peck at and nibble its small costume jewels.
She pronounces on the pros and cons of clipping
"pinions versus broadspans.
If you do it wrong, they fly up,
then drop like a stone."
(Do it right and they're lateral thinkers.)
"*And*," she exults, "they'll soon be able to talk.
They're both so used to the subway,
I should do commercials for the TTC!"

Racing home in an SUV
what cell-phoned commuter
is granted this full measure?

Rebel Armies

In this refugee camp, at the centre of the gang,
a thickly muscled seven-year-old soldier
they call Mike Tyson, after the boxer/rapist,
holds the stance of a guard dog.
His shaved scalp is cross-furrowed with scars,
his eyes round with baby paranoia.

The rebel armies in his country prize children
for carrying out orders without question
to amputate captives' hands and feet.
(One slender teen protests he refused at first,
till his own legs were part of the bargain.)

Think, too, of the youth of Palestine
who in a deadly ballet
use metaphoric slingshots to dodge army bullets.

Early morning's a time to avoid the mirror
that lights the face as only its owner notices,
the separating baseboards, sagging soffit of skin.
Yet it also reminds of a former therapist
who wore optimism like a thick beefsteak strapped to his chest,
and the plucky blind lady from the Islands
who, when helped to negotiate the intersection at Vaughan,
protested, "Soch a beezy street, this won,
and everywon een a horry..."

By nightfall
these players will line up in parade,
to be reviewed like a cast of confused seniors
who "sundown" in a busy nursing home.
Some staff, a youthful counselor, perhaps,
will attempt to console "survivors":
It wasn't your fault,
you did what you had to do to survive;
if only you'd had a choice,
or real opportunities...

But a few residents shuffle on,
and one mumbles,
Phooey. What does *he* know
from death camps...

Fancy Wedding

When so many out-of-towners RSVP'd "Yes"
the guest list underwent a generational divide
and only one small child made the final cut.
But don't children make or break a marriage?

Grown up, how many fewer might choose
to marry outside the faith
if granted the chance to marvel at
the magic of the *chupah* canopy,
the hand-painted *ketubah* contract,
the orbiting ritual, and the groom
smashing a glass underfoot
to remember the great ruined Temple?
At what price, the seamless video
interrupted by the crying
of only a solitary bridesmaid?

In the ballroom
there awaits a sumptuous meal
and heartfelt speeches from soulmates
from the early years.
A dance floor features a seven-player, four-figure band.
As they strike up the *hora*
the bride and groom are beckoned onto chairs
then hoisted aloft by cherished friends,
soaring within inches of the hotel's
bulbous modern chandelier,
far out of reach of the one small child.

High School Concert

After the work day, our mad scramble
to find the auditorium, catch what's left,
leads us past rustic murals dedicated
to the fallen young of both great wars.
We've missed the welcoming Fiesta Nueva,
but take our seats as overly resonant
cannons rattle in the Britannia piece,
then drown in thunderous applause
when the short perspiring teddy bear in black
turns to take his bow.

There he is, in the first row, our own boy,
strawberry-tipped spikes on a chemical blonde.
It must be hot for him under those high beams,
down here too, as mothers fan with their programs.

Twin Oprahs, emcees Letisha and Temika
alert us to get out our Kleenex for the lovely vocal quartet.
Its "For the Beauty of the Earth"
and spirited sentiments from *Les Miz*
seamless as poured coffee
could make a disgruntled poet cry.

Such transformations:
these offspring with posture straightened
dipping into classical wells we nearly lost;
the kid with Tourette's syndrome
squeezing his twitchy restlessness
through a trombone's bell;
a wistful loner chiming in briefly on xylophone;
a strapping brush cut crashing cymbals
who's being scouted by the National League;
and a lovely graduand on a flute solo
too perfect for band classes alone.

To all the wonderful parents
who drove these kids in the wee morning hours,
Thank you, chime Letisha and Temika.
(Our own boy woke himself at six a.m.,
made breakfast, and scanned the sports page
before he left us still in our bed.)

There he is, the one with the wildest hair,
strawberry-tipped spikes on a chemical blonde,
seated in the front row, but wisely taking his place
in the musical background, on unfaltering clarinet,
foot tapping time, enjoying, we suspect, as we do,
the sheer counting exercise of it all.
It's a peppy civility, counterpoint to the pastoral murals
and the fallen young of both great wars.

R.D. Laing

Into the Glaswegian staidness of our psychiatry centre,
seminar room adoring with trainees,
came Ronnie (my namesake) Laing
of apostolic hairline and oracular eyes,
the slight man who recast schizophrenia
from a chasm to a plateau
where its sufferers looked down with a terrible status.
Author of *The Divided Self,*
his own Scottish childhood barren and cold,
his topic that day was "Birth Trauma"
begun in a defensive brogue:
There'rr those who accyooz me of bein' an anti-psycheye-iatrist,
But in feck, nuthin' coold be ferrther from th'trooth.

Beside him sat Dr. Gordon, late of the UK,
whose coal-miner build had burrowed
to full professorship and could crush
Laing with a single blow,
whose beefy arm
only ten minutes into the talk
as the great man began uncontrollably to sob,
and the rest of us froze in silence,
reached out to comfort.
"There, there, now. It'll be all right."

Master of "inner self versus outer,"
Laing shook off the hug,
and invoking the patron saint of peaceful birth Fréderik Leboyer,
soldiered on, almost an hour.

"What d'they groo on th'stony soil o' Scotland?"
—the old joke—"They groo *men*!"
Yet here was one such man
from across the stormy Atlantic
showing us that greatness can unravel
like three-ply tissue,
to honour an illness
people would rather dismiss
and delivering us
from illusions of invincible fame
with his own full-throated cry.

Appelfeld

At a grand conference to honour Aharon Appelfeld,
Israeli novelist of Holocaust Aftermath,
three panelists discussed the great man's work.
One, sweet-looking as an elderly Jewish mother,
was a septuagenerian from Montreal
who wrote epic Yiddish novels.
Why, she asked, before a packed house,
were all his books approximately 200 pages in length?
Why did he present concentration-camp survivors
as empty and depraved?
Why were so few healthy Jewish women portrayed?
Why was the most marriageable woman in *The Conversion*
a Christian who kept house in a Jewish home
who, in charge of the Jewish rituals,
became more Jewish than her employers?
Could Mr. Appelfeld—may he enjoy 120 years of life—
not do any better than that
by his own people?

A hush fell at the surprise attack
on a man who had crossed an ocean
to speak to us, to teach,
a Jewish writer of more than a dozen novels
worthy of a Nobel Prize,
all of them read by so many seated.

Beside her on the panel,
the youthful Yiddishist shook his head.
The greatness, the universality
of works such as *Badenheim 1939!*
A masterpiece! It had stunned him into awareness
of his own calling as a Jewish writer.

Third on the panel, a psychiatrist/orator,
stared the old woman down.
In Appelfeld's books, he insisted,
the absence of horrific Holocaust detail
was akin to the great speeches in tragedies
by couriers who recount events
too horrible, too profane to demonstrate,
all the more real for that fact.

At the end of the discussion,
slight, balding, the giant
Appelfeld rose from his seat
and thanked the panel by gently retelling
a priceless anecdote from the repertoire
of Reb Nachman of Bretslav:

A king and his first minister
learned that this year's crop of grain
would make everyone in the kingdom mad.
The minister urged that he and the king
eat only of last year's.
"Let the people eat of the deadly crop."
But the king said, "No,
we must join them in partaking of it.
But we will paint a sign on each other's brow,
so that every time we look at one another,
we will know that we are insane."

Indeed, the epic novelist had been dead wrong,
grinding her own axe at Appelfeld's expense.
He might have asked,
"Why did you want to read
the book I *didn't* write
when you can write it yourself?"

And yet, what will be the reaction
to the portraits of empty, depraved survivors
by readers who know little, if anything,
who never spoke to anyone
directly or even indirectly
touched by that Horror?
As slowly the pen turned in my hand,
in its frail girth I felt
an easily hidden
dagger.

VISITATIONS

Last night I awakened to pounding at my door
and a menace of infectious laughter.
It was The Coach, with eight strapping kids,
and my son the group was after.
All had hazel eyes and sandy hair,
and wore uniforms with a Gothic "D"
on the back, a corporate logo.
I tried to feign no surprise.
"It'd be a shame," he said,
"if an athletic kid like yours
never got a chance to play.
We practice Friday nights. Games are on Saturdays.
If he trains really hard, one day it just might pay."

As soon as they left, I fell back into dreaming
only to wake to a ballet troupe
come to carry off my daughter.
There were willowy girls with graceful necks and limbs
costumed in black Danskins and pink pointe shoes.
"The Dance," said the Artistic Director, "is a Tree of Life.
It would be a shame if an elegant girl like yours
missed out on the pirouette and *le grand* jeté.
If she's devoted, she'll one day hold the stage.
We rehearse in the Church daycare up the street
on Friday nights. We perform on Saturdays."

In a sweat I lurched up from a nightmare
to still more knocking at my door.
This time it was a tall Young Rabbi
who carried an enormous book.
He too had come for my children.
"It would be a shame," he said, "if bright kids like yours
missed out on a chance to pray.
Our services start on Friday nights.
The devout come also on the Sabbath Day."

I asked him to set down his book,
but he gave me a look of pity,
his eyes grown heavy-lidded
as he transformed into The Old *Rebbe* in a Greatcoat.

I stammered, invited him in for a *glayzeleh tay*,
I sensed he might be the prophet Elijah
or some other Messianic *geist*.
But as I backed into the house
my head was deep in uneasy sleep,
and I was fading fast in the eyes
of zealots who know where my family lives,
and who always come to play.

Reading Layton on the Subway

Unfazed by the feeling "too Jewish"
I consider a poetry book for the subway,
an oracular proclamation by Klein or Dudek, Mandel or Mayne,
the less ethnic stylings of Waddington or Michaels,
perhaps an honorary Jew, or was-married-to-one,
like Roo Borson, or Heather Spears,
or an ethnic hybrid-with-a-difference,
a gurufied L.A. Montrealer
named Cohen.

This morning "The Bull-Calf" rides on my lap
even as "Keine Lazarovitch" blazes in my mind,
"how She loved God but cursed extravagantly all his creatures."
For a moment I see what became of
the Lazarovitch *bocher*,
"lord of all the marquees"
with "a mind full of goats and pirates
and simpler than a boy's,"
like those dark-eyed Barneys and Bernies and Barrys
all named for the Hebrew *baruch*,
who poured their blessed sweat like workahol
into the public and private good,
sharing with the world their brilliance *and* their spleen,
a perverse brood
more determined to excel
than fit in.

Things slow into focus.
I see writing on the wall, swiftly stand
and wind my way.
In the train doors my reflection looks harrowed and severe,
a male version of Keine Lazarovitch, *alev hasholem*,
(She would have scared me senseless,
much as Layton did his motion-sick son.)
As I cross the gap and the doors close behind
and the train recedes north to suburbia,
may I offer the finest compliment
a fellow exile can drop:
Irv! You almost made me
miss my stop.

Immersion

I

Fashioner of sparse lines, dreamer of postcard stories,
a poet reading a novel is hard to miss.
He leans forward so far
lugubrious eyes stick on dense passages
from which he must gingerly pull away.
Through setting, action, and character,
he plods, even as the plot line demands
the reader pick up the pace.
Sometimes deeply he sighs, and scratches
his greying temple, submerged
in the rivered sweep of prose.

II

A middle-aged poet waits with two rabbis
behind a screen of painted concrete-block
while his young wife-to-be recites the blessings
for ritual immersion,
a second baptism to re-form her
from Christian to Jew.
She is slow to emerge,
keeps the next two converts waiting.
Fearing emotion has caused the delay
the poet jokes with his age-mate, the Senior Rabbi:
"If my partner were now Orthodox,
she could just slip a wig
over all that damp hair..."
The rabbi smiles.
"She's *not* planning to wear a *sheytl?*"
To impress the learned man,
the poet dusts off his Yiddish:
Ess dacht zich mir az der sheytl gehert zum shtetl.
(It seems to me the ritual wig belongs in the *shtetl.*)
The rabbi shakes his greying head,
re-immersing them all:
Der shtetl iz umatum.
The shtetl is everywhere.

Epilogue:
Thank You

Thank You

Dear gnarly-fingered lady
with the yellow-gray hair
who scales the fifteen stairs
to our doctor's by sheer will,

in the waiting room you scan *Time* and *Life*
with a magnifying glass and light
while we secretly look on,
already feeling healthier.

A Brief Glossary of Non-English Terms Not Translated in the Poems

p. 8 *Malleus Maleficarum*: (Latin) a Fifteenth Century treatise on witchcraft, demonology and criminal procedure.

vers libre: (French) free verse.

p. 27 mishkin... prince: after the saintly protagonist in Dostoevski's novel *The Idiot*, Prince Mishkin.

p. 29 *Il Duce*: (Italian, pron. eel dootshay) literally "The Leader," a title assumed by the dictator Benito Mussolini prior to the Second World War.

p. 37 *babushka*: (Ukrainian) literally "kerchief," an affectionate term for an elderly Slavic woman.

p. 44 *tsunami*: (Japanese) a series of undulations in the sea caused by earthquakes or other seismic disturbances; often misnamed "tidal waves."

p. 50 *tabernacle!* : (French) a blasphemous expletive, after the niche or receptacle for Eucharistic elements.

p. 55 *klayner:* (Yiddish) literally "little one," sometimes used as a nickname for the penis.

p. 57 *shiksa*: (Yiddish, after the word for "blemish") a pejorative term for a non-Jewish woman, especially one who is young and alluring to young Jewish men.

*goya: (*Yiddish, literally, a female "of the nations") a pejorative term for an older non-Jewish woman; sometimes used to refer to a cleaning-lady.

Anti-Semeet: ("Yinglish"): an emphatic Yiddishized pronunciation of "anti-Semite."

p.65 *erhu*: (Chinese) a two-stringed musical instrument played with a bow; produces a peaceful or mournful sound.

mon semblable, mon frère (French): translates to "my likeness, my brother," from Baudelaire's preface to *Les fleurs du mal,* quoted by T.S.Eliot in "The Wasteland."

p.74 *glayzeleh tay*: (Yiddish) little glass of tea.

geist: (Yiddish) spirit.

p. 76 *bocher*: (Yiddish, pron. with a gutteral "ch"): a male youth.

p. 77 *baruch*: (Hebrew) blessed.

alev hasholem: (Hebrew) may (s)he rest in peace.

p. 78 *sheytl*: (Yiddish) a ritual wig worn by Orthodox women for reasons of propriety.

shtetl: (Yiddish) in the narrow sense, an Eastern European village inhabited by Jews; in the broader sense, a place where poverty and persecution were endured through religious devotion and shared community values; as chronicled in the fictional works of Sholem Aleichem, on whose Tevye stories the musical *Fiddler on the Roof* was based.